Henry Parry Liddon

The Whole Counsel of God

The Duty of the Clergy as Teachers of the People

Henry Parry Liddon

The Whole Counsel of God
The Duty of the Clergy as Teachers of the People

ISBN/EAN: 9783337160005

Printed in Europe, USA, Canada, Australia, Japan

Cover: Foto ©Lupo / pixelio.de

More available books at **www.hansebooks.com**

The Whole Counsel of God:

OR, THE DUTY OF THE CLERGY AS TEACHERS OF THE PEOPLE, WITH PARTICULAR REFERENCE TO THE RECENT JUDGMENT IN THE CASE OF "ESSAYS AND REVIEWS."

A SERMON

PREACHED IN

THE ABBEY CHURCH OF ST. MARY, SHERBORNE,

ON THE

SECOND SUNDAY IN LENT, FEB. 21, 1864,

AT THE GENERAL ORDINATION OF THE

LORD BISHOP OF SALISBURY.

BY

HENRY PARRY LIDDON, M.A.

STUDENT OF CHRIST CHURCH; ONE OF THE SELECT PREACHERS AT OXFORD AND EXAMINING CHAPLAIN TO THE LORD BISHOP OF SALISBURY.

PUBLISHED BY REQUEST.

SECOND EDITION, REVISED.

OXFORD & LONDON,
RIVINGTONS:
OXFORD,
JOHN HENRY AND JAMES PARKER.
1864.

TO THE REVEREND THE CLERGY ORDAINED AT THE ABBEY CHURCH OF SHERBORNE, ON THE SECOND SUNDAY IN LENT, 1864, THIS SERMON, PUBLISHED AT THEIR REQUEST, IS DEDICATED WITH SINCERE AFFECTION AND RESPECT BY THEIR BROTHER AND SERVANT IN JESUS CHRIST.

The Whole Counsel of God.

ACTS xx. 27.

I HAVE NOT SHUNNED TO DECLARE UNTO YOU THE WHOLE COUNSEL OF GOD.

HERE is one of those passages in the New Testament, which make a forcible and direct appeal to the heart and conscience of every man who has undertaken or is undertaking to serve God in Holy Orders. The words occur in that parting charge to the Presbyters of the Church of Ephesus, which on the eve of his going up to Jerusalem, at the close of what is termed his third Missionary journey, the great Apostle delivered on the strand at Miletus. They are such words as escape men at the turning points of life, at entering upon or taking leave of great responsibilities—compressed, fervid utterances of the deepest thought and of the strongest currents of feeling—of thought and feeling which for the moment will not be pent up and restrained within the barriers of ordinary habit, or of studied reserve. Even a saint may, nay, at certain times, he must speak of himself: and so the great Apostle glances hastily at the labours and sufferings which had marked his sojourn at Ephesus[a]. Then he points anxiously to the lowering future: he tells his hearers the precise limits of his supernatural knowledge. The exact

[a] vers. 18—21.

form of each of the many trials before him he did not know; but he knew generally, that in every city bonds and afflictions awaited him, and in particular, that he and they to whom he spake would meet again in this world no more[b]. Under the pressing urgency of this conviction, he predicts the coming sorrows of the Church of Ephesus—the Church indeed of St. Timothy and of St. John, but also the Church of men who denied the central truth of the Resurrection[c]; the Church of Hymenæus, and Philetus and Alexander; the Church of the Nicolaitans, whose morals were hateful (we are told in the Apocalypse) to the Lord Jesus[d]; the Church, as it might seem from St. John's first Epistle, of some of the earliest heretics, who denied the real Union of Godhead and Manhood in our Lord and Saviour[e]. Indeed, only a few years later, we see in the two Epistles to Timothy the clear traces of an organized opposition to Christian truth at Ephesus, so formidable in its various intellectual activities, that the stern energy of the Apostle's language in the speech before us is only understood when read by the light of a struggle, unlike to, and in some respects more serious than, any other within the limits of the Apostolical Age.

Casting his eye over this troubled future, St. Paul utters a prophecy of mournful solemnity. 'I know this, that after my departing shall grievous wolves enter in among you, not sparing the flock. Also of your own selves shall men arise, speaking perverse things to draw away disciples after them[f].' He

[b] vers. 22, 25.   [c] 1 Tim. i. 20. 2 Tim. ii. 17, 18.
[d] Rev. ii. 6.   [e] 1 St. John iv 2, 3.   [f] Acts xx. 29, 30.

exhorts them to watch : he commends them tenderly to God : but he also recalls to them the full measure of their personal responsibility. His ministry had put them in entire possession of the truth as it had come from heaven : and, if they fell into the snares which lay thick around their future path, they could not, when facing the knowledge and the justice of God, attempt to shelter themselves under the plea of ignorance. 'I take you to record this day, that I am pure from the blood of all men. For I have not shunned to declare unto you, all the counsel of God[g].'

The whole counsel of God! Such is the Apostle's expression for that fixed body of Truth, which we of this day name more commonly the Gospel, the Revelation of Christ, the Faith of Christians. St. Paul says, that he had declared the whole mind—that is, the whole revealed mind—of God. Observe, of God. His language excludes that conception of religious truth which makes it merely the product of the truest, purest, deepest thoughts of the highest and largest minds among the sons of men. "Flesh and blood" had not revealed to St. Peter the dignity and the claims of Jesus[h]. "Flesh and blood" added nothing to that Revelation of His Son which the Eternal Father had made to the soul of St. Paul[i]. Resting on a Divine Authority, and being human only so far as was necessary, if it was to close with the intellect and the heart of man,—human in its condescensions and human in its sympathy, but in its truth and essence Divine—the Gospel was for St. Paul unlike any other object-matter that entered into his thought. It was

[g] vers. 26, 27. [h] S. Matt. xvi. 17. [i] Gal. i. 16.

sundered by a broad line of demarcation from all else that seemed like it on this side or on that; it did not shade off into any either of the higher philosophies or of the less sensual idolatries, of the time. So absolutely and exclusively true did he deem this Gospel-truth to be, that could an Angel from heaven have been conceived as preaching any other, the Apostle would unhesitatingly have held him "accursed[k]."

The whole counsel of God! It was God's word, not man's; it was neither the result of a thoughtful speculation, nor yet an approximative guess, nor yet a cunningly devised fable. Being God's word, it was as a *whole* worthy of the best thought and love that His creature could give it. That ministry of three months in the great Ephesian synagogue[l], and then the two years which followed of laborious teaching in the School of the Rhetorician Tyrannus[m], and last, but not least, the wide publicity, the general attention[n], and the active hatred of heathen foes which culminated in the Riot of the Amphitheatre[o], had enabled the Apostle to put forward the Gospel, the whole area of its Doctrine, the many sides on which it attracted, and awed, and subdued the soul of man—in unabridged unmutilated completeness. 'All they which dwelt in Asia (i. e. Asia Minor) heard the word of the Lord Jesus, both Jews and Greeks.'

This solemn and momentous day, may be the very crisis of their destiny to those of us who are waiting to receive a Commision from heaven, at the Altar

[k] Gal. i. 8.   [l] Acts xix. 8.   [m] Acts xix. 9.
[n] Acts xix. 10. 17. 20.   [o] Acts xix. 23—41.

of this noble Minster. And the words of the Apostle may serve us well, as a guide to our thoughts, our aspirations, our resolves. These time-honoured walls cannot but recall to a stranger some of the most cherished memories of the Anglo-Saxon Church[p]; while in their renewed beauty they speak not less persuasively of the renovated life of the modern Church of England. Can we forget to-day that wellnigh eight centuries have passed since here at Sherborne the Commission of Christ was handed on by a predecessor of our Chief Pastor to those who in the early ages of our national history sought to serve God within the precincts of the Sanctuary? How vast, we feel, is the life of a Church, when contrasted with the fleeting existence of her members: yet how insignificant, when we place it side by side with the Being of her Everlasting Lord! His Person, His Word, the Laws of His Kingdom and of His Service, the results of His doctrine upon the soul of man, are at this hour what they were at the first, what they will be to the end of time. And if instead of losing ourselves in vague reflection, we would give a practical turn to our (it may be) somewhat eager tide of thought and feeling, let us fix our attention on this primal, this simple duty of an ordained man—the declaration of the whole counsel of God. When St. Paul asserts that he has not "*shunned*" to declare it, the English word, and yet more strongly[q] the original for which it stands,

[p] Cf. Handbook to the Abbey Church of St. Mary Sherborne, by the Rev. E. Harston, pp. 32—38.

[q] ὑπεστειλάμην, cf. Meyer in loc. Dr. Wordsworth sees in it a nautical metaphor, which might have been suggested by the scene before the speaker.

must remind us that there are many motives and hindrances calculated to keep a man back from doing that which must be done, if he fears his God, if he cares for his own soul, if he has any true love for the souls of those to whom of his own free will he undertakes to minister.

1. Now one cause of failure in this primary duty would seem to lie in a lack of religious knowledge. It is much more easy to be deficient in essential knowledge of religious truth than we are apt to assume. I do not contemplate the extreme case of ignorance, whether this or that doctrine does or does not lie within the limits of Revealed Truth. For it would be simply immoral in a Christian Teacher not to have learnt the frontier and outline of that sacred deposit of the Faith which our Lord and Saviour has committed to His Church to hold fast and to hand on to the end of time. But far short of this extreme shortcoming, may we not too easily acquiesce in an ignorance which is scarcely less fatal to souls? May we not lapse into a habit of thinking and speaking of the doctrines of the Gospel, as if they were like soldiers in a regiment,—so many units, each adding something no doubt to the collective bulk and area of Doctrine, while yet in no way essential to its organic completeness, and therefore each capable of being withdrawn, without inflicting any more serious injury upon the entire truth than that of diminished size? Do we not hear persons talk of the articles of the Creed in this way,—as if each article was a perfectly separate and new truth,—as if each was, I might almost say, a

new and gratuitous infliction upon the reluctant intellect of man,—as if each was round and perfect in itself, and had no relations whatever to any truth beyond it? Yet what does such language really prove but defective knowledge in those (be they who they may) who use it? They "know" the doctrines of the faith only as so many separate propositions. Of the Great Whole, which lies beyond the words, and the several sides of which the words do at best but imperfectly represent,—of the Body and Substance of the Faith, they know little or nothing. They fail to perceive the connexion, the interdependence, the organic unity of all truth that rests on the authority of God. Their view is too superficial to enable them to do justice to that marvellous adjustment of truth to truth, of faculty to object, of result to cause, which is a direct and obvious perception to souls who gaze prayerfully and steadily at the complete Revelation of Christ. These really shortsighted persons do not miss a revealed doctrine which is withdrawn; nor are they offended when a human speculation is elevated to co-ordinate rank with the certainties of Faith. It seems to them to be merely a question between more or less belief; between a larger or a smaller creed; between, as they would speak, a greater or a less number of dogmas. But in reality, each truth, touches, implies, has relations to, truths right and left of it; and these relations are so intimate and so vital, that no truth can be withdrawn, and leave conterminous truths intact. The Faith is, if I may say so with reverence, so marvellously compacted, so instinct with a pervading life, as to resemble a natural organism, I had almost said a living creature. Just as St. James says of the moral law, that he who offends in one point is guilty of all[q], because of the unity of the impaired principle; and as St. Paul teaches, that in the body of the Church, if one limb or member suffer, all the members suffer with it[r], in virtue of an internal and necessary sympathy; so in the Creed, no one truth can be misrepresented, strained, dislocated, much less withdrawn, without a certain, and frequently an ascertainable injury resulting to other truths which are supposed to be still unquestioned and intact. For there are nerves and arteries which link the very extremities of Revealed Doctrine to its brain and heart; and the wound which a strain or an amputation may inflict, must in its effects extend far beyond the particular doctrine which is the immediate seat and scene of the injury.

This power of perceiving and exhibiting the deeper internal relations and grounds of Christian Doctrine might seem to correspond to that "word of knowledge" (λόγος γνώσεως,) which in his catalogue of the gifts of the Spirit St. Paul distinguishes from the "word of wisdom" (λόγος σοφίας)—the faculty of stating the truths and mysteries of the faith in clear and precise language[s]. It is to be won

[q] St. James ii. 10.   [r] 1 Cor. xii. 26, 27.

[s] σοφία nämlich ist die höhere christliche Weisheit (1 Cor. ii. 6.) an und für sich, so dass Rede, welche die Lehrstücke (Mysterien) derselben ausspricht, klar macht, anwendet, u. s. w., λόγος σοφίας ist. Damit ist aber die tiefdringende erkenntniss dieser Lehrstücke, die speculative Erfassung und Einsicht und Verarbeitung ihres Zusammenhangs, ihrer Gründe, ihrer tiefern Ideen, ihrer

partly by the culture and exercise of the sanctified intellect in study, partly, nay rather specially, by prayer for illumination and a habit of meditation on Scripture and the Creeds. There are eminent exercises of this gift within the limits of inspiration. St. Paul's demonstration of the fatal antagonism of the practice of circumcision to true belief in our Lord's redemptive work, in the Epistle to the Galatians, will naturally occur to us. Of uninspired instances I may refer to that masterly and well-known account of the connexion between the doctrine of the Sacraments and the doctrine of the Incarnation, which the English Church owes to the mind, and which she studies in the language of the great Hooker.

When a man possesses this gift of knowledge—of 'knowledge' in the technical sense of St. Paul—he will teach the whole truth not by an effort or mechanically, but in virtue of an instinct. He will be carried forward, from principle to application, from centre to circumference, from the heart and brain of doctrine to its utmost extremities; because he sees, he cannot but see, its evident, its organic unity; because to mutilate it would be to him scarcely any thing short of a moral and intellectual agony. A living faith, informed by study, and quickened and stimulated by prayer, can hardly be guilty of accidental, never of culpable reticence; it cannot but 'declare the whole counsel of God.'

Beweise, ihrer Ziele, u. s. w. noch nicht gesetzt; eine Rede aber, welche sich damit beschäftiget, ist λόγος γνώσεως. Meyer in 1 Cor. xii. 8.

2. A second hindrance is lack of courage. To speak for God to man,—for the just and holy God to man sinful and wilful in his sin—requires nerve and courage. To represent God as He is—as just no less than merciful, as punishing sin no less certainly than rewarding faith and holiness—this, to be done well and honestly, requires courage. Moses before Pharaoh, Samuel before Saul, Micaiah before Ahab, Jeremiah before the Princes of Judah, St. John the Baptist before Herod Antipas, St. Stephen before the Sanhedrim, St. Paul before Felix and Agrippa, and (in a sense altogether peculiar, and unrivalled,) Our Divine Lord before the Jewish Priest and the Roman Magistrate—these represent the attitude and the fortunes of truth at the bar of human nature. Human nature indeed is wretched, and it craves for comfort—that, my clerical brethren, that is our opportunity[t]; but it is also proud, and it resents humiliations, aye and it is strong, and likely, in its own fashion and way, to express its roused resentment. Of old they understood this well, who went forth uplifting the cross, while yet baring their breasts to death. They knew that the patient to whom they were carrying the medicine that would cure him would often refuse the draught, and would punish the physician who dared to offer it. But they loved man, and they loved and feared their God too sincerely and too well, to infuse new ingredients, or to withdraw any of the bitter but needful elements of cure. They accepted civil and social proscription; they endured moral and physical agony; they embraced, one after another, with

[t] 2 Cor. i. 4.

cheerful hearts, the very warrants and instruments of their death,—because they had counted the cost, and had measured too well the greatness of their task, and the glories of their anticipated eternity, to shrink sensitively back at the first symptoms of opposition, or of difficulty. St. Paul might have foreseen the conduct of Demetrius, and the tumult in the amphitheatre; but this was no serious reason for considering the worship of Diana as a sort of modified or imperfect revelation, or as any thing short of a hateful lie[u]. He did not shrink from declaring the whole counsel of God.

If I yet feared men, says the Apostle, I should not be the servant of Christ[v]. The man who is not in very deed emancipated from bondage to any human fear, cannot do justice either to the needs of his fellow-men or to the Rights of God. He cannot be loyal to Truth. There are petty oppositions, petty persecutions, indirect yet powerful influences, which will stay a man's hand, and silence his tongue, even in this age and land of civil freedom; unless his conscience be quick and his will strong, through a constant sight of One Who is the Lord and the Subject of that Truth which He proclaims. He will abridge, soften down, mutilate his message, unless he have penetrated the certainty that the fear of man bringeth a snare[x]—

---

[u] St. Paul's speech at Athens recognizes that element of natural Religion which is at the bottom of all superstitions however debased. What the Apostle really thought of the Paganism of the Ancient World as a whole, is best understood from such passages as Rom. i. 23—32.
[v] Gal. i. 10.   [x] Prov. xxix. 25.

to all indeed who would serve God in sincerity of purpose,—to none, with such fatal and destructive results, as to the man who undertakes to serve Him in the Christian Priesthood.

3. The want of spirituality of heart and soul is a third cause of defective representation of doctrine. To speak for God to the souls of men, a man must himself, in his inmost soul, have consciously stood face to face with that truth of which he speaks[y]. He must speak *of God* as one who has known at once His dread awfulness and His tender love; *of sin*, as that which he feels to be the one master-evil, and with which as such he has struggled in good truth within his secret self; *of Christ*, His Person, His propitiatory and atoning Death, His life-giving Sacraments, as of the Person and Acts of a dear Friend, loved with the heart's warmest and best affection, which yet adored with the deepest homage and by the chiefest powers of his prostrate spirit;—*of Eternity* as of that for which he is himself making daily solemn preparation;—of *prayer, and the care of conscience* and the culture of purity and truth within, as of things of which he knows something by trial and exercise, perhaps even something more by failure. Himself a redeemed sinner speaking to sinners who need or who have found their Redeemer, he will speak in earnest. The issues of endless life or endless death may hang upon his words; but his strength must lie in the profound conviction that he is but the instrument and organ of One Whose livery he wears before the eyes of men, and without whom he can do nothing.

[y] St. John i. 1—3.

Christian Preaching may be defined either as Speaking for God, or as Speaking to souls: but whichever definition a man keeps most prominently before him, he must aim in the pulpit at making a spiritual as distinct from a merely literary effort. Above him is the Father of Spirits, dwelling in light which no man can approach unto. Before him is the human soul, strong, subtle, intricate, with untold capabilities for good and evil, for joy and agony. Surely he cannot but keep close to those great truths which warm the heart and nerve the will, and raise the whole spiritual being from sin to holiness, from death to life, from the miseries and degradations of mere nature to the sanctities and magnificence of grace. But if the preacher should himself stand outside the spiritual life; if prayer, communion with God, discipline of the will, culture of the affections,—if these things should seem to him but an extravagance or a fanaticism, and if the Faith of the Church be only lodged in his understanding, as an important fact in the history of opinion, or as the bare result of an arithmetical calculation; then it is not difficult to see how he will presently fail, as a matter of course, to declare the whole counsel of God. His thought will drift naturally away from the central and most solemn truths to the literary embellishments which surround the faith; he will toy with questions of geography, or history, or custom, or scene, or dress; he will reproduce with vivid power the personages and events of long-past ages, it may be with the talent of a master-artist; he will give to the human side of Religion the best of his time and of his toil. In doing this he may, after the world's measure, be doing good work; but let us not deceive ourselves —he will not be saving souls. Souls are saved by men who themselves count all things but dung that they may win Christ, and be found in Him[z]; and who, even if they be men of refined taste and of cultivated intellect, know well how to subordinate the embellishments of Truth to its vital and soul-subduing certainties. Especially if a man should take refuge in the literary aspects of Scripture, because he is not sufficiently assured of its leading truths to reproduce them with the accent—the accent which the people understand so perfectly—of simple unfaltering conviction; then the contrast between his graceful but relatively useless disquisitions, and the glorious Creed of the Church of God—which in its integrity alone responds to the profound yearnings of the soul—will be painful in proportion to the opportunities which he has missed, and to the powers which he has abused.

4. Once more; here, as in the whole field of ministerial labour, let a man work and pray for the grace of an unselfish spirit. Let him endeavour to strangle the love of self by the love of God and the love of man. For without charity, though a man should speak with the tongues of men or of angels, he will do nought for the real good of his hearers, or for the glory of his Lord. Selfishness will spoil everything. How often are not we, the Representatives of Christ, constrained to rebuke ourselves, humble ourselves, condemn ourselves, by the words which we speak from the Chair of Truth! Some there have been who have yielded to the fatal temptation of being, what they call, consistent. They tone down

[z] Phil. iii. 8.

God's message to the miserable level of their own felt shortcomings. They make of the Gospel a Gospel of acquiescence in sin, rather than a Gospel of redemption from it; they profess to see in it a patronage of the flesh, and a recognition of the world, I had almost said, a co-partnership with the Evil One. Alas! who can doubt, that unless a man can speak, in simple sincerity, as for Christ and from Christ,—careless though his words should only reach his people at the manifest expense, nay, through the deep humilation, the self-inflicted, self-adjudged penance of their Minister—it must needs go hard with him hereafter in the day of account. Better it surely were never to speak at all, than to make the Lord of Purity and Light a seeming accomplice in the crime and darkness of His creature! far better were silence than the advocacy of an impoverished—a mutilated—a false Gospel—a Gospel robbed of all that is mysterious, awful, supernatural, divine; because forsooth, to preach the perfect Truth which came from heaven is unbecoming for one who lives, and who feels that he lives, as if it were not true! Even the double-hearted prophet, who knew that he had much to win by falsehood, could not but tell the Pagan King, who would fain have subsidized his inspirations, 'Whatsoever the Lord telleth me, that will I speak[a].' And can we, beneath the Cross of Christ, so pander to self, as to " handle the word of God deceitfully?" Dare we say less than what we know to be Truth, because we know also that Truth in its fulness would be our condemnation?

Or take another illustration of the need of an unselfish spirit. It is possible, nay probable, that

[a] Numb. xxii. 38; xxiii. 12. 26; xxiv. 13.

we may have what are called favorite doctrines, sections or sides of Truth through which God has in a special sense spoken to us, moved us, sanctified us, (as we trust) saved us. Of these, no doubt we can speak with more power, because with more intimate perception of their bearing on the secret springs of life and death. But we also speak of such points with less of moral and intellectual effort than of others; and this greater facility is likely to be the real cause of our giving them an undue prominence in our cycle of teaching, while we endeavour to whisper to our consciences, and to persuade our friends, that these points are the essentials of the Gospel, and that all the rest is comparatively unnecessary. Thus men teach the Atonement, and ignore the Sacraments; or they teach the need of faith, and ignore the need of love and holiness; or they teach the beauty of our Lord's character, and forget His Propitiatory and Sacrificial Death; or conversely, they insist upon the outward duties of religion, and do scant justice to the spiritual and internal forces of the soul. We must teach *all* that God has revealed, because He has revealed it, leaving it to Him to touch one soul by this, and another soul by that portion of His Revelation. Even within the limits of inspiration, St. Paul preached faith, and St. John love, and St. James practical energy, each giving prominence, (but nothing more) to these several sides of the Christian life, while yet each preached it as a whole. No man of modesty and thoughtfulness would make the narrow circle of experiences that have passed within his own soul, the absolute standard of the truths and powers which may act on others: and no duty is more difficult or more serious than that of detaching ourselves from the influence of "favorite doctrines," and, as far as may be, teaching the whole truth in its integrity to all to whom we owe it, as the gift of God. And the Proper Lessons and Epistles and Gospels of the Church Service, enable us to correct our natural tendency towards a choice of texts and subjects which fall within our own more contracted area of thought and feeling: so that in making it a rule always to preach from the Services of the Day, or at least on a subject suggested by the season, we make provision against one of the chief temptations to teach something less than the whole counsel of God. Nothing, however, but a spirit of genuine self-sacrifice, nothing but a true love of the souls of men, can enable a man so to forego his own predilections, so to throw himself into the state of mind, and points of view, and peculiar difficulties, and narrower or broader horizons of his hearers, as to lose himself, and the little history of his own spirit, in the mighty work of proclaiming in its perfectness the Truth of God. We know how the great Apostle combined this perfect consideration for others, with an unflinching, chivalrous loyalty to the claims of Truth. "Though I be free from all men, yet have I made myself servant unto all, that I might gain the more. And unto the Jews I became as a Jew, that I might gain the Jews; to them that are under the Law as under the Law, that I might gain them that are under the Law; to them that are without law, as without law, (being not without law to God, but under the law to Christ,) that I might gain them that are without law; to the weak became I as weak, that I might gain the weak; I am made all things to all men, that I might by all means save some[a]." How could self-sacrifice be more unsparing? By whom could the duty of declaring the whole counsel of God be more forcibly proclaimed, than by a man who gave up all else to enable him to discharge it?

Under ordinary circumstances, my brethren, it might be natural at this point to leave the principles which have been insisted on to your mature reflections, and to the obvious force of their intrinsic truth. The duty before us is sufficiently plain; and the risk of wearying you might well lead me to pause, if it were indeed possible to do so. But I yet owe something to the promptings of conscience, and to the Rights of God. Nor would your judgment be harsh or unreasonable, if you should interpret my silence as to a matter of pressing and public anxiety, as something less easily to be pardoned than mere failure to satisfy the many claims of this great occasion. Such silence would in fact be nothing short of notorious treachery to the whole spirit and drift of those kindling words, which it has been my endeavour to recommend and illustrate.

At no age of the Church could the ambassadors of Christ have afforded to forget the Apostle's example of "not shunning to declare all the counsel of God." But never was the force of that example more needed than in our own day. Illustrations indeed press so urgently upon the mind, as it ranges over the recent history of the Church, that the preacher's

[a] 1 Cor. ix. 19—22.

embarrassment lies in the very liberty of his choice: but one illustration, I doubt not, will have occurred to many of us living at this time, and living, my Lord Bishop, under your Lordship's jurisdiction, in this your Diocese of Salisbury, with painful but irrepressible prominence. My brethren, it would be an affectation, if I should profess to suppose you ignorant of a recent Judgment, proceeding not indeed from a spiritual but from a temporal court; which, although it professes, and that eagerly[b], to avoid all attempts at formal determination of doctrine, yet does unquestionably determine the *legal* sense and value of doctrinal formularies, and, as doing this, has and must have, practically and morally, no little weight with large classes of our countrymen. That Judgment would seem, among other points, to have ruled, that it is permissible in law for a clergyman to express a "hope" for the final restoration of the lost. No man can know any thing of his own sinful heart who does not know how much there is within him which is ready to welcome such a permission; but the question is a question not of the inclinations of a sinful creature, but of the Revealed Will of a Holy

[b] "With respect to the legal tests of doctrine in the Church of England, by the application of which we are to try the soundness or unsoundness of the passages libelled, we agree with the learned Judge in the Court below that the Judgment in the Gorham case is conclusive:—This Court has no jurisdiction or authority to settle matters of faith, or to determine what ought in any particular to be the Doctrine of the Church of England. Its duty extends only to the consideration of that which is by law established to be the Doctrine of the Church of England, upon the true and legal construction of her articles and formularies." Judgment (Guardian, Feb. 10, 1864.)

God. May we, consistently with That Will, indulge that "hope?" Assuredly not. For nothing is more certain than that by the terms of the Christian revelation any such hope is delusive and vain, since it is opposed to the awful Truth, that they who die out of favour with God and are lost, are lost irrevocably, lost for ever. If Holy Scripture is still to be our Rule of Faith, Scripture, I submit, is decisive. If Hooker's well known caution as to the interpretation of Scripture, " that where a literal interpretation will stand, the farthest from the letter is commonly the worst" is still to be kept in mind, that rule will preclude any serious doubt as to the real mind of Scripture in this solemn matter. Scripture is no less explicit as to the endlessness of the woe of the lost soul, than as to the endlessness of the scene or instrument of its punishment. Isaiah speaks of the 'everlasting burnings[c],' Daniel of 'everlasting contempt[d],' our Lord of 'the everlasting fire' once and again[e], St. Paul of 'everlasting destruction' or ruin[f], St. Jude of 'a blackness of darkness which is reserved for ever[g].' Three times speaking of the penal woe of the lost, the Apostle of Love uses an expression of energetic redundancy and force: he says that it lasts 'unto ages of ages[h].' Just as the

[c] מוֹקְדֵי עוֹלָם Is. xxxiii. 14. [d] דִּרְאוֹן עוֹלָם Dan. xii. 2.
[e] τὸ πῦρ τὸ αἰώνιον, Matt. xviii. 8; xxv. 41.
[f] ὄλεθρον αἰώνιον, 2 Thess. i. 9.
[g] Οἷς ὁ ζόφος τοῦ σκότους εἰς τὸν αἰῶνα τετήρηται. Jude 13.
[h] The smoke of their torment ascendeth up for ever and ever, εἰς αἰῶνας αἰώνων, Rev. xiv. 11; εἰς τοὺς αἰῶνας τῶν αἰώνων, Rev. xix. 3, and Rev. xx. 10. The language of Isaiah from which this is taken would certainly seem to refer to a more than temporal judgment on Edom and other nations. Is. xxxiv. 9, 10.

elect will reign in heaven for ever and ever[i], as holy souls desire that God may be glorified for ever and ever[k], as Jesus Risen from His grave is alive 'for evermore[l],' as in His glory He shall reign for ever and ever[m], as the very Life of God Himself is described by saying that 'He liveth for ever and ever[n],' so is this same measure applied to the punishment of the lost souls[o]. Are we to say that a period of limited duration is all that is meant to be ascribed in Scripture to the glory of the blessed in heaven, to the Glorified Life and Reign of Jesus, to the very self-existent Life of GOD Himself, in order to enable ourselves to rest in the conception of a Purgatory beyond the Final Judgment, as less shocking to our 'consciousness' than the Belief in Hell? And if not, can we certainly determine that as applied to Hell, this phrase has an altogether narrower sense than that which we ascribe to it in such passages as apply it to Heaven or to the Reign of Christ? Modern scepticism has tampered with the word "Eternal," just as it has emptied 'Salvation,' 'Atonement,' 'Grace,'—nay the very Name of God Himself, of their natural meaning. But "everlasting" means neither more nor less that than which lasts for ever. True indeed it is that the Hebrew expression which, when applied to future time, answers to the English 'for ever,' does in particular instances mean something less than boundless duration. But this is the case only where a limitation is forced upon the word by the subject to which it is applied. Originally the word does imply indefinite,—the nearest

---

[i] Rev. xxii. 5.   [k] 1 Tim. i. 17. Heb. xiii. 21, &c.
[l] Rev. i. 18.   [m] Rev. xi. 15.   [n] Rev. iv. 9, 10; v. 14; x. 6.   [o] Ubi sup.

approach, perhaps, which the human mind can make to infinite,—extent of continuance. Taken at its lowest range of meaning, it means an existence co-extensive with that to which it is applied [p]. In the New Testament, there is a substantive which varies with the various meanings of this Hebrew word [q]; but there is also an adjective derived from that substantive, which at least, as used in the New Testament, does not so vary [r], but means what we

[p] עוֹלָם, properly that which is *hidden*; as applied to future time, that which is lost to sight in the distance. Instances of the narrow range of the word may be found in Gen. ix. 12. Ex. xii. 14—17; xxvii. 21; xxviii. 43. Lev. x. 15, &c. Not however in such passages as Ps. xlv. 7; lxxii. 5. 17; lxxxix. 37. where Rationalists limit the word in deference to their own prejudices against the Messianic predictions. Nor again in salutations 1 Kings i. 31; Neh. ii. 3; Dan. ii. 4, &c. since in these cases, the true force of the expression is to be measured by the belief of the Jews in the immortality of the soul. Of what range of meaning the word is really capable will be best understood from a consideration of the following extract from Gesenius: " vera æternitatis notio in vocabulo nostro iis in locis inest, qui immortalem summi Numinis naturam spectant, quod, vocatur אֵל עוֹלָם Deus æternus Gen. xxi. 33; Jer. xl. 28. חֵי הָעוֹלָם in æternum vivens Dan. xii. 7. (cf. חָיָה לְעוֹלָם vivere in æternum, immortalem esse instar deorum [Dei] Gen. iii. 22. Job vii. 16), Cui tribuuntur זְרֹעוֹת עוֹלָם brachia æterna Deut. xxxiii. 27. et de Quo dicitur אַתָּה אֵל וְעַד עוֹלָם מֵעוֹלָם Ps. xc. 2, ab æternitate ad æternitatem, Tu es Deus. Ps. ciii. 17. cf. Ps. ix. 8; x. 16; xxix. 10; xciii. 2." Thesaurus sub voc. עלם.

[q] αἰών. Although, as Bretschneider remarks, " partim Græcorum more usurpatur." Like עוֹלָם its original meaning was that of unlimited duration, and the narrower senses were imposed upon it subsequently. " Aristoteles alicubi scripsit αἰών dici quasi αἰὲν ὤν." Vorstius Hebraism. N. T. ii. 39.

[r] That in the LXX, αἰώνιος like αἰών, when applied to future

English mean by "everlasting." And it is this last-named word which is used in the passages principally under discussion. If it should be precariously contended that this word implies positive endlessness of continuance, as little as it admits of any defined limitation of continuance: it may at least be observed, that as used in Scripture of the penal misery of the lost, the expression 'eternal' is fixed in the sense of endless duration by two considerations. Where that word is applied to our home in Heaven,

time, varies in its meanings with the senses of עולם is clear from the passages given in Tromnius, s. v. But, when the Gospel had "brought life and immortality to light" more distinctly, the use of the word αἰώνιος was limited (within the precincts of the New Testament) to the idea (taken at the lowest) of indefinite continuance. It is used seventy-one times in the N. T. It is an attribute of ζωή forty-four times. St. John never uses it in any other connection; and it occurs twenty-three times in his writings. In two cases only is it possible to argue fairly that the word *may* have a limited meaning. (1) Philemon 15. αἰώνιον αὐτὸν ἀπέχῃς, where however Bretschneider (Lex. Man in voc.) construes the word "illum in sempiternum, scilicet, quia Christianus factus jam vitæ æternæ particeps erat." So (to omit others) Huther in loc. "Die christliche brüderliche Verbindung in die Ewigkeit reiche." (2) St. Jude 7. πυρὸς αἰωνίου δίκην, where Pol. Synops. in loc. observes that the natural construction of the whole passage is that " Eas urbes incensas instar exhibere ignis æterni, qui impios expectat." The remarks of Huther apply to our E. V. πυρὸς αἰωνίου construiren De Wette, Arnaud mit den folgenden δίκην ὑπέχουσαι, weil dieses sonst zu entblösst stände: allein das Feuer, womit sie bestraft sind, konnte von Judas nicht wohl *das ewige Feuer* genannt werden; dies ist stehende Bezeichnung des Höllenfeuers, dem die im letzen Gerichte Verurtheilten überliefert werden; darum ist es besser πυρ. αἰων. mit δεῖγμα zu verbinden; jene Städte sind δίκην ὑπέχουσαι ein Exempel des Ewigen Feuers. Brief des Judas. p. 217.

the hopes and longings of men gladly do justice to the natural force of human language. But it is noteworthy[s], that no stronger expressions are applied any where to the Eternal Life of the Blessed in Heaven, within the New Testament, than are also used to describe the endlessness of the pains of Hell[t] : and therefore the notion that

[s] αἰώνιον in N. T. 2. dicitur omne quod est finis expers, maxime id, quod est post hujus vitæ mundique decursum eventurum. Huc pertinent omnia illa N. T. loca, in quibus formulæ : πῦρ αἰώνιον, κρίσις αἰώνιος, κρίμα αἰώνιον, κόλασις αἰώνιος, ζωὴ (δόξα, σωτηρία) αἰώνιος reperiuntur, v. c. Matt. xviii. 8. xix. 16. xxv. 41. 46. Marc. iii. 29. Rom. ii. 7. 2 Tim. ii. 10. Heb. v. 9. Quemadmodum enim formulis πῦρ αἰώνιον et sqq. pœnæ perpetuæ peccatorum, quas impii post hanc vitam luent, *sorsque eorum misera futura non interrupta* indicantur, ita opposita formula : ζωὴ αἰώνιος perennis felicitatis piorum post mortem status et conditio significatur, quæ 2 Cor. iv. 17. αἰώνιον βάρος δόξης, Luc. xvi. 9. σχηναὶ αἰώνιοι, Heb. ix. 15. αἰώνιος κληρονομία, et 2 Pet. i. 11. αἰώνιος βασιλεία τοῦ Θεοῦ appellatur. Schleusner. Lexicon. p. 67. So too Bretschneider (Lex. Man. in v.) who after quoting all the passages in which the word αἰώνιος is applied to blessedness or woe, observes, ' Αἰώνιος in formulis ζωὴ αἰων. πῦρ αἰων. δόξα αἰων. κόλασις, ὄλεθρος, κρίμα, κρίσις αἰων. *sempiternum nunquam finiendum* indicare dubio caret, quum præmia æque ac pœnæ post resurrectionem sempiternæ quoque haberentur a Judæis. Vid. test. Aser. in Fab. Cod. Pseud. V. T. i. p. 693. potissimum Psalter. Salom. Ps. 3. vers. 13. 15, 16. ubi ἡ ἀπώλεια τοῦ ἁμαρτωλοῦ εἰς τὸν αἰῶνα ; piorum ζωὴ αἰώνιος autem, οὐκ ἐκλείψει ἔτι. p. 31.

[t] Commenting on the use of αἰώνιος in St. Matt. xxv. 41. 46, with reference to endless life and endless death, St. Augustine observes : " Si utrumque æternum, profectò aut utrumque cum fine diuturnum, aut utrumque sine fine perpetuum debet intelligi. Par pari enim relata sunt, hinc supplicium æternum, inde vita æterna. Dicere autem in hoc uno eodemque sensu, vita æterna sine fine erit, supplicium æternum finem habebit, multùm absurdum est. Unde, quia vita æterna sanctorum sine

of the two states Heaven only is endless, finds no support from the language of Scripture, but rests solely upon a human speculation external to it. On the other hand, 'eternal' is not the only attribute applied in the New Testament to the state of punishment: the word is illustrated and defined by other terms which necessarily fix its true meaning. The Baptist speaks of the penal fire as 'unquenchable[u].' Our Lord Himself adopts the word; He thrice said of the "worm" of a sinful conscience that "it dieth not," and that "the fire" of its punishment "is not quenched[x]." The prophet, whose language is quoted, had used a *future* tense[y], the Divine Speaker, before whose Eyes the unseen world is spread out—on this side in all its unspeakable Beauty, on that in all its unutterable Woe—uses a *present*, as describing the fact yet more vividly. If endless punishment could be described in human words, no words could exhaust the description more absolutely than the recorded words of Christ. They admit of no limitation; they are patient of no toning down or softening away; in the page of the Evangelist, they live for all time before the eyes of men, in all their vivid, awful power. If Jesus Christ has told us any thing certain about the other world,

---

fine erit, supplicium quoque æternum quibus erit, finem procul dubio non habebit." De Civ. Dei, xxi. 23. Even Hagenbach, who quotes this passage, observes : " It is superfluous to quote other Fathers, inasmuch as they all more or less agree." Hist. Doct. vol. i. p. 387.

[u] πῦρ ἄσβεστον. Matt. iii. 12.

[x] εἰς τὸ πῦρ τὸ ἄσβεστον· ὅπου ὁ σκώληξ αὐτῶν οὐ τελευτᾷ, καὶ τὸ πῦρ οὐ σβέννυται. Mark ix. 43, 44. 46. 48.

[y] וְאִשָּׁם לֹא תִכְבֶּה, Is. lxvi. 24.

we can not doubt that the Penal fire must last
for ever. But may the soul be withdrawn from the
punishment? or may it be annihilated? Few
Christians have dared to say 'yes' to the first of
these questions; to the second, fewer still. For
there are Words of Christ which seem expressly
designed to prevent any misconception. He speaks
of a 'punishment,' no less than of a 'fire,' which is
"everlasting[y]." And we are told, that as " he that
believeth on the Son hath everlasting life;" so "he
that believeth not the Son shall not see life, but
the wrath of God abideth on him[z]." " Abideth

[y] St. Matt. xxv. 41. 46. After noticing the classical distinction
between κόλασις and τιμωρία, (Ar. Rhet. i. 15. Plat. Prot. 323, e.)
Archbishop Trench observes, (Synon. N. T. i. p. 28.) "It
would be a very serious error, however, to attempt to transfer
this distinction in its entireness to the words as employed in
the New Testament. The κόλασις αἰώνιος of Matt. xxv. 46, as it
plainly itself declares, is no corrective and therefore temporary
discipline; it can be no other than the ἀθάνατος τιμωρία (Josephus,
B. J. ii. 8. 11), the ἀΐδιοι τιμωρίαι (Plato, Ax. 372, a), with which
the Lord elsewhere threatens finally impenitent men (Mark ix.
43—48); for in proof that κόλασις had acquired in Hellenistic
Greek this severer sense, and was used simply as punishment
or torment, with no necessary underthought of the bettering
through it of him who endured it, we have only to refer to such
passages as the following: Josephus, Ant. xv. 2. 2; Philo, De
Agricul. 9; Mart. Polycar. 2; 2 Macc. iv. 38; Wisd. of Sol.
xix. 4. This much, indeed, of Aristotle's distinction still
remains, and may be recognised in the sacred usage of the
words, that in κόλασις the relation of the punishment to the
punished, in τιμωρία to the punisher, is predominant."

[z] John iii. 36, ἡ ὀργὴ τοῦ Θεοῦ μένει ἐπ' αὐτόν. Compare the
Psalmist's, צַד־נֵצַח לֹא יִרְאוּ אוֹר (xlix. 20.) with the earlier part
of this text. The true force of these words can only be set
aside by the a priori and unwarrantable assumption that the

on him;"—then if he die in unbelief, he still *exists*, though in his woe—then he is *not delivered* from it. "Abideth on him:" the piercing words seem to ring on from day to day, from year to year, from century to century, from cycle to cycle of measureless periods; we feel at this moment that eighteen centuries have not blunted their edge, or lessened their solemnity and power. If so (you reply), it were better never to have lived, than to live and be lost. Unquestionably. Our Lord states this truth with equal clearness. He said of one lost soul, of one who had been blessed with the high privilege of His Companionship, but who fell so deeply as to betray Him to His enemies for money, 'Good it were for that man if he had never been born[a].' There are undoubtedly critics who treat these words as they might treat an exclamation in some heathen Dramatist; as if the sentence had been uttered in a free rhetorical spirit, and with no thought of the meaning—the vast illimitable meaning —which they really contain and convey. But you can only thus empty the Words of Christ of their native power, if you will consent to forget that they are the Words of One Whose horizon was not bounded by the things of time. The Lord of Life and Death, fixing His Eye in deepest woe, yet with unfaltering precision, upon a creature whom He willed to save, yet who spurned His Salvation—thus rules in the fulness of His knowledge, in the tenderness of His Love, that non-existence had been better than an

endless life of the soul was a truth unknown to the Hebrew Psalmists. Compare König. Theologie der Psalmen, p. 329 sqq.
[a] St. Mark xiv. 21. Compare St. Mark iv. 29, and viii. 36, 37.

undying being, which in the abuse of its free-will His creature had made an unending misery. It cannot be maintained that the Words of Jesus are true, if at any conceivable point of a distant future any restoration to heaven is possible for Judas. For beyond that point, however distant, there would still stretch the vision of a still illimitable Eternity; in which the restored soul would find in the presence of God, a "fulness of joy" which would redress the balance, and would speedily reduce a purgatory that had lasted even for ages to a scarcely perceptible speck in a past existence. Unless the human soul be not necessarily immortal, Judas lives: unless the Words of Christ be untrustworthy on the question of Life and Death, Judas lives in woe. There is no escape: the unspeakable awfulness of our Saviour's language is precisely *this*, that it does leave no room for any reversal of the doom of the betrayer—of the man whose epitaph was thus traced by the finger of Infinite Knowledge and of Infinite Love,—" Good were it for that man if he had never been born."

A few gifted minds such as Origen[b] have made

---

[b] The passages which best illustrate his deliberate opinion are in formal treatises, (De Prin. i. 6. Contr. Celsum, v. 14, 15.) In his popular teaching, he sometimes expresses opinions which seem to foreshadow the later Doctrine of a purgatory before the Judgment, (Hom. vi. in Exod. no. 4. Hom. iii. in Ps. xxxvi. no. 1. quoted by Lumper 9. 595.) or which at least say nothing inconsistent with it. He admitted however that his doctrine of a final ἀποκατάστασις (of men and devils) might be dangerous to the unconverted. 'For most,' he says, 'it is enough to know that sinners will be punished. It would be inexpedient to say more: since there are persons whom the

shipwreck, from whatever causes, of this Article of the Christian Faith. But amidst the rare aberrations of genius, the belief of the Christian people has been such as might have been expected, from the tenor of the Words of Christ. And it is particularly observable how in the early ages of the Faith, the martyrs standing before their heathen judges, felt one after another that their choice lay between a transient pang of suffering and an endless woe[c]. Not that the error which is connected with the name of Origen has been repudiated by no process less rude and irregular than the action of popular sentiment. Apparently during his life-time and certainly after his decease, the speculations of the great Alexandrian were condemned by councils of the Church[d]; and if

fear of Eternal Punishment scarcely restrains from giving themselves up to wickedness with all the evils that follow on it!" Contr. Cels. vi. 26. He speaks of belief in eternal punishment as morally useful although not true, (Hom. in Jer. 19. tom. iii. p, 507, 508. ed. Migne) when commenting on Jer. xx. 7, thus admitting the adaptation of the Revealed Truth to the wants of the human soul. This conviction seems to have coloured his popular teaching. (Hom. 7. in Exod. Opp. ed. Migne, vol. ii. p. 347, where he quotes Is. lxvi. 24.)

[c] Ruinart Acta Sincera. Passio Stæ Felicitatis (p. 23.) circa 150. Passio S. Maximi, circa 250 (p. 133.) Maximus is described as a plebeian who was engaged in trade. When desired by the Proconsul to sacrifice, that he might escape the torture, he replied, "Hæc non sunt tormenta quæ pro nomine Domini nostri Jesu Christi inferuntur, sed sunt unctiones. Si enim recessero a Domini mei præceptis, quibus sum de Evangelio Ejus eruditus, vera et perpetua mihi mane bunt tormenta." Other examples might be cited from Ruinart: they shew what was the simple, unhesitating faith of the Early Church.

[d] Origen was silenced and deposed by two successive synods

equivocal language on the subject of endless punishment is to be discovered in a stray writer here and there by the student of Patristic Literature, he will almost invariably observe that its force is destroyed by language of an opposite drift, which the same writer has elsewhere employed. Nor is it pretended that there is any serious ground for doubt as to the Catholic Belief of the Church, as evidenced by the consent of her Representative Fathers[e]. But, let us note it well, they who to-day deny the truth in

held during his life-time. His leading tenets were condemned at Constantinople in 540. "The erroneous doctrines (says Archdeacon Churton) which Origen had taught, or which others taught in his name, were condemned as heretical; and among them the doctrine of the future restitution of fallen spirits and of evil men. See this very fully proved by a Church Historian, who has given it the fullest examination. *Natal. Alex. Hist. Eccl. Sæc.* iii. Diss. xvi. And this is admitted by the best-informed enquirers of our own Church, as by those of foreign Churches. See Bishop Pearson, Minor Works, i. 413. and the able Life of Origen in the venerable Archdeacon of Westmoreland's *Biographies of the Early Church*, ii. 114. 133." (Guardian, March 9, 1864.) To the objection that Origen was not condemned by any of the First Four General Councils, it has been well replied, "that each Council did the special work of its own emergency, and not other kinds of work; and that Origenism was not a pressing question in 325, 381, 431, or 451." (W. B. in Guardian, March 16, 1864.) It is at least certain that the Sixth General Council declares the Fifth to have assembled for the purpose of condemning Origen and other persons, thereby endorsing the anathema of the Synod of Constantinople in 540. (Routh. Script. Eccl. Opusc. ii. 232.)

[e] See Petavius de Angelis, lib. iii. c. 8. It will be observed that Petavius quotes language from Gregory of Nyssa, and Gregory Nazianzen, which may fairly outweigh those passages of doubtful import in their writings, to which appeal has recently been made.

question, or who rashly express "hopes" that the Faith of Christendom may not be true, oppose themselves not merely to the decrees of Councils and to the consent of Fathers, nor yet merely to the 'popular' belief of centuries, nor to the reign of a world-wide Tradition. Nor do they merely controvert a Hebrew Prophet or a Christian Apostle, and take up the position of those inconsequent Rationalists, who, respecting nothing else in Holy Scripture, still profess to respect as Divine and Infallible the recorded Words of Christ. For it is face to face with Him that they stand in controversy[f]: it is His sentence, in Whose disclosures concerning the world beyond the tomb, we Christians place our hopes for life and for death, that they arraign at the bar of what is at best a section of contemporary opinion. Our Lord and Saviour, with what would be generosity in a mere man, but with what in Him doubtless was provision against the known weakness of His creatures, has not bequeathed to His Servants or Representatives the responsibility—

[f] Observe the force of the following admission from a writer, of whose relations to the true Faith of the Church of Christ no unfair estimate will be formed from the fact of his being one of the five authorities referred to with approbation by M. Renan, in his recent "Vie de Jesus." (Int. p. vii.) M. Reuss has been citing St. Matt. xxv. 30. 41 sqq. and some similar passages: "Toutes ces peintures," he says, "sont claires et simples; elles n'offrent rien d'équivoque; il n'y a pas un mot qui trahisse une arrière-pensée, qui nous fasse entrevoir une signification cachée, qui les réduise à une valeur purement figurée et parabolique. Il est évident que les narrateurs qui nous servent ici de guides, ont pris tout cela au pied de la lettre et qu'il ne leur est pas resté une ombre de doute à cet égard." Reuss. Theol. Chrétienne, tome i. p. 249, Deux[me] edit.

nay the odium—of proclaiming those stern and awful certainties; He has Himself heralded, at one and the same time, the penalties and the benedictions of His Gospel; He has unveiled the Eternal Pit Himself, in phrases and words as urgent and positive as those whereby He has opened heaven to all believers; and fifty generations of Christians have believed and confessed that His Authority is final, and that to tamper with His Revelations is only more obviously foolish than it is perilously blasphemous.

Brethren! I seem to interpret to myself the thought of your hearts: men are won, you say, by the mercies rather than by the terrors of the Lord. Would it not be more accurate to say with St. Augustine, that the terrors of the Lord drive us men to take refuge in His unspeakable mercies? Is it not a fact, familiar to every clergyman, is it not a matter of personal experience to some at least in this vast congregation, that the undefined, haunting fear of an endless woe does again and again guide unquiet souls to seek peace and safety in kneeling at the foot of the Cross, and in tasting of that Plenteous Redemption, which flows from the Wounds of Jesus? Are there not now resting in Paradise souls, who owe their predestined crowns and thrones to that first sharp pang which pierced their spirits, when, many years since, on earth, in the midst of a course of sin, they first realized the certain existence of an endless Hell? You urge that there are higher motives than terror, for religious effort. Undoubtedly. It is better to love God for His own sake, than to love Him for the sake of the blessings which He gives, or the woes from which He saves. But He who made the human heart knew more perfectly what motives are really needed to act upon it, than the theorists who proclaim what they would propose as the revision of His work. He knew that more men are moved by fear than by love : and that man may be educated to love fearlessly, if he begins by cultivating that fear which is the beginning of moral and spiritual wisdom. Certainly we cannot exaggerate the mercies of our redeeming Lord : they are simply infinite. But side by side with them lie also His judgments, unexplored and infinite; so that the 'great deep' is their symbol in the world of nature ; and His judgments are equally with His mercies an integral part of the Truth of His Revelation, nay of His Being : they are equally a part of His 'whole Counsel' as it has been made known to us men; and it is our business, as clergy, to proclaim them. To do so, many of us solemnly pledge ourselves this day before God and man. We owe it, my brethren of the laity, to our God ; we owe it to Jesus Teaching and to Jesus Crucified; we owe it to the terms of our commission, and to the claims of our consciences ; but we owe it above all to your undying souls to tell you the plain, unmutilated truth. We dare not, like the serpent in Paradise, whisper to you here within the precincts of the Church of God, that you may cherish a 'hope' that God's threats may after all be false. To tell you that in the future world the only alternative to Heaven is a Purgatory, might indeed earn for us, at the present crisis of thought in England, a momentary popularity. But if it were morally in our power to sacrifice one truth of the Creed, we could not thereby insure the rest. We could not stop at "expressing a hope" that the punishment of the wicked may not be final. On the one side, an Eternal Heaven might easily become both to the philologists, and to the metaphysicians, as problematical a thing as an Eternal Hell. On the other, that infinite Price which our Lord paid upon the Cross that He might save us from a boundless woe, would soon be rejected as needless; and we should reduce His propitiatory Sacrifice to the level of a moral triumph. From that it were but a short step to the denial of His Godhead. For, as a perfect act of faith in a single truth has already, before perceiving it, grasped other truths by implication; so a deliberate rejection of a single truth entails the rejection, first in principle, and afterwards avowedly of other truths beyond. Here is our danger. Fear you we may not: but you may shame our weakness by bidding us tell you the truth, or you may tempt us in speaking to you, to "prophesy smooth things,' or at best to substitute the 'hay, wood, and stubble' of the things of time, for the unchangeable realities of the other world. If we dare not be honest with you; if through want of spirituality, from a selfish instinct that we should condemn ourselves in your eyes, we should shrink from a high and soul-controlling doctrine—woe, woe to us! One day we know side by side with you, but with greater, far greater responsibilities than yours, which we have freely chosen to bear, we too, your ministers, must stand at the Judgment Seat of Christ. How shall we then make answer to the stern and terrible rebuke of our Master, how shall we endure to hear your deserved reproaches, your wail of remorse and agony, if now, through cowardly fear of man, or any false refinement, or weakly acquiescence in the polished unbelief of the hour, we hide from you one half of our Master's message; justifying by our silence the taunt of His enemies, that in this age we fear to preach what He Himself announced as certain; or banding ourselves with them, in saying that He was at least in part mistaken, and that the men of to-day have improved His Gospel by eliminating its severities?

And you, my dear brethren, who now are pressing forward to receive your various powers from the consecrated Hands through which to-day, as ever before and to the end of time, Christ our Lord reigning in His Church bestows them—bethink you, I pray, at this the most solemn crisis of your lives, of that great Day which cannot be distant, and which may be very near. Bethink you now, as you receive your talent of the account which you must then render for its due improvement. Pray that you may be fearless, as speaking for the Mighty God; but pray too that you may be loving, and humble, as becomes sinners, who remember their own sins, while in God's name they dare to counsel their brethren. If we of the Clergy feel in our very hearts that we may be lost, as easily, nay rather, by reason of our greater opportunities, much more easily than other men; we shall speak of Hell, not as a threat which we flourish without measuring its awfulness, but as a fact, present to the eye of our spirits; we shall think and speak of it as of a common danger—just as of Heaven as of a common Hope, and a common Home. Let us by God's grace resolve to be true; let us pray God to make us true—true in our inmost selves—and true to that counsel of God, which it is our duty to proclaim to man. God indeed is severe and stern with the self-reliant; but for the self-distrustful and the prayerful He is a tender and most indulgent Master, whose service is not less the highest joy, than it is the highest freedom. Even on earth for every earnest, simple, truthful, unselfish spirit among the servants of the Church, there is a foretaste of the imperishable Reward above. It may be enjoyed, and that abundantly, in the cottages of the poor, in the pulpits of the Sanctuary, on the steps of the Altar. Stephen may still ennoble the lower grade of service by a sacrifice of self which opens heaven, and which Jesus owns as the first of martyrdoms. And there are mercies, blessings, crowns that fade not away[f]—for those who though afar off, yet by word and act, faithfully witness to the justice and to the grace of their God, and who standing beneath the Cross of the Redeemer of the world, wield, according to the measures of their ministry, the consolations of the keys of Peter, the powers of the sword of Paul.

[f] 1 St. Peter v. 4.

APPENDIX.

The following Litany has already been offered to the public in another shape. It is here reprinted by the permission of its Compiler,—the revered Author of the Christian Year. The fulness with which it exhibits the mind of Scripture as to the solemn question of Eternal Punishment, will remind the reader how much of the Scriptural argument has been left altogether untouched in the pages of my Sermon. The Litany is little less than the skeleton of a treatise; and can hardly fail to convince fair and reasonable persons that the truth recently impugned is an essential feature of the Teaching of our Divine Lord. But the cause of truth will be best promoted, and the Compiler's intention most strictly complied with, if the Litany be used, and that frequently and earnestly, in the manner suggested by its name and form.

H. P. L.

Litany of our Lord's Warnings.

I.

O God the Father, King Eternal, Immortal, Invisible,

O God the Son, Redeemer of the world, begotten from everlasting of the Father,

O God the Holy Ghost, Eternal Spirit, proceeding from the Father and the Son,

O Holy, Blessed, and Glorious Trinity, Three Persons and One God, Which is, and Which was, and Which is to come,

—Have mercy upon us.

Remember not, Lord, our offences, nor the offences of our forefathers; neither take Thou vengeance of our sins: spare us, good Lord, spare Thy people, whom Thou hast redeemed with Thy most precious blood, and be not angry with us for ever.

Spare us good Lord, and be not angry with us FOR EVER.

II.

§ 1. JESU, Who of old didst reserve the fallen angels in everlasting chains under darkness unto the judgment of the Great Day,— *S. Jude 6; 2 S. Pet. ii. 4.*

JESU, Who to our fallen parents didst declare Thyself the true and just Judge, and didst condemn them for listening to him who said, "Ye shall not surely die," *Gen. iii. ver. 17.*

JESU, WORD of God, by Whom the old world was, and was destroyed by water, and the world that now is is reserved unto fire for perdition of ungodly men, *2 S. Pet. ii. 5; iii. 6.*

JESU, LORD, Who from the LORD didst rain brimstone and fire out of heaven on Sodom and Gomorrha, and didst set them forth for an example, suffering the vengeance of eternal fire, *Gen. xix. 24; S. Luke xvii. 20; 2 S. Pet. ii. 6; S Jude 7.*

JESU, Who in the figure of Esau hast taught us that there may be a condition where is no place for repentance, *Heb. xii. 17.*

JESU, Who by Thy Prophet hast told us of everlasting burnings, *Isa. xxxiii. 14.*

JESU, Who by Thy Forerunner hast threatened unquenchable fire, *S. Luke iii. 17.*

§ 2. JESU, from Whose lips, full of grace, came thrice the terrible mention of "the whole body cast into hell," *S. Matt. v. 29; xviii. 8.*

JESU, Who didst bid us fear Him which is able to destroy both soul and body in hell, *S. Matt. x. 28; S. Luke xii. 4.*

JESU, Who didst warn us against a relapse which should make the last state worse than the first, *S. Matt. xii. 45; S. Luke xi. 26.*

JESU, Who didst tell us over and over of the furnace of fire, and of the outer darkness, where is weeping and gnashing of teeth, *S. Matt. xiii. 42, 50, &c.; viii. 12, &c.*

JESU, Who didst declare it possible for a man to "lose his own soul," *S. Matt. xvi. 26; S. Mark viii. 36.*

JESU, to whom the foolish virgins will come asking for entrance in vain, *S. Matt. xxv. 1—12.*

JESU, Who by one and the selfsame word, "everlasting," hast described the sentence both of bad and good, *S. Matt. xxv. 46.*

JESU, Who didst mention not only the worm and the fire, but *their* worm and *their* fire,—what *each one* suffers,—as undying, *S. Mark ix. 44, 46, 48; cf. Isa. lxvi. 24.*

—*Have mercy upon us.*

LITANY OF OUR LORD'S WARNINGS. 39

JESU, Who vouchsafing to interpret Thyself, hast declared, that Everlasting Fire means the Everlasting Punishment of those who shall be on the Left Hand,

§ 3. JESU, Who in tender love didst say to Judas, "Good were it for that man if he had never been born," S. Matt. xxvi. 24.

JESU, Whose own word it is, "He that believeth and is baptized shall be saved, but he that believeth not shall be damned," S. Mark xvi. 16.

JESU, Who hast told us of the Resurrection of damnation, as well as of the Resurrection of life, S. John v. 29.

JESU, of Whom we have learned that a man may become as a devil, S. John vi. 70.

JESU, Whose threat it is, "Ye shall die in your sins;" and "Whither I go ye cannot come," S. John viii. 21, 22.

JESU, Who likenest them that abide not in Thee to a withered branch whose end is to be burned, S. John xv. 6; Heb. vi. 8.

JESU, Who by Thy Apostle hast taught that to some the Gospel is as a savour of death, 2 Cor. ii. 16.

JESU, Whose revealing from heaven shall be everlasting destruction from the Presence of the Lord to them that obey not the Gospel, 2 Thes. i. 9.

JESU, Who tellest the Hebrews of some that cannot be renewed unto repentance, Heb. vi. 4—6.

JESU, from Whom final impenitence can look for nothing but "fiery indignation," Heb. x. 27.

§. 4. JESU, Who by two of Thy loving Apostles speakest of some for whom "the mist of darkness is reserved for ever," and of "a latter end worse than the beginning," 2 S. Pet. ii. 17, 20; S. Jude 13.

JESU, in Whose presence the worshippers of the Beast shall be tormented with fire and brimstone, Rev. xix. 20.

JESU, Who hast ordained that the smoke of their torment, as the smoke of Babylon, should go up for ever and ever, Rev. xiv. 12; xix. 3.

JESU, Who didst shew to Thy loving Disciple how those not written in the Book of Life shall be cast into the lake of fire, Rev. xx. 15.

—Have mercy upon us.

Rev. xxi. 8.	JESU, Who didst cause the Father's voice to be heard, saying, "The cowardly, and the unbelieving, and the abominable, and murderers, and whoremongers, and sorcerers, and idolaters, and all liars, shall have their part in the lake which burneth with fire and brimstone, which is the second death,"
Rev. xxi. 27.	JESU, into Whose city none shall enter that defileth, or worketh abomination or a lie, but they that are written in the Lamb's Book of Life,
Rev. xxii. 11.	JESU, some of Whose last words were, "He that is filthy, let him be filthy still;" his probation having come to an end,
Rev. xxii. 16.	JESU, from Whose home the unclean, the cruel, the profane, the false will be finally excluded,
Rev. xxii. 12.	JESU, Who art coming quickly, and Thy reward with Thee, to give every man according as his work shall be,

—*Have mercy upon us.*

III.

From everlasting damnation :

From all blindness of heart :

From contempt of Thy word :

From self-will and self-reliance; from going after our own inventions; from following a multitude to do or believe evil :

From wresting Thy Holy Scripture; from mistrusting Thy holy Church; from bigotry and indifference; from partiality and prejudice; from respect of persons; from making God's Word of none effect by man's tradition :

From hastiness and sloth; from presumption and cowardice; from levity and scornfulness in judgment, and from taking part with the scorners :

From the sullenness of Cain; from the unbelief of Sodom; from the bitter and tardy cry of Esau; from the hardness of Pharaoh; from the self-deceit of Balaam; from the relapsing of Ahab; from the despair of Judas; and from the portion of the devil and his angels :

—*Good Lord, deliver us.*

From the lake that burneth with fire and brimstone, which is the second death:

In the time when iniquity aboundeth; in the days when the Son of Man shall hardly find the faith in the earth; in the revelation of Antichrist; in the hour of our own death; in the passing away of heaven and earth; and in the eternal judgment:

—*Good Lord, deliver us.*

IV.

We sinners do beseech Thee to hear us, O Lord God; and that it may please Thee to restore unto thy Church perfect unity both visible and invisible:

That it may please Thee to look down with pity upon the Reformed Catholic Church in the British Empire, in its long and sore distress by reason of unhappy divisions:

That it may please Thee to grant unto our Bishops and Pastors and all congregations committed to their charge, so to cherish the bond of peace, that they may not in any degree forfeit the unity of the Spirit:

That it may please Thee to fill the successors of the Apostles with the spirit of power and love and of a sound mind, that by the Holy Ghost so dwelling in them they may keep Thy good deposit both of doctrine and Sacraments:

That it may please Thee to bestow on our gracious Queen Thy special grace, that she may be crowned hereafter as a true Defender of the Faith:

That it may please Thee to endue those who make our laws, and judge in our courts, with a true sense of the mind of Thy Church, as well as with a spirit of equity as between man and man:

That it may please Thee to give unto us all a right judgment and a steady and courageous will, faithfully and lovingly to hold fast Thy form of sound words, not in the letter only but in the spirit:

That it may please Thee to make our hearts silent and submissive for the unreserved receivings alike of Thy promisings and Thy threatenings:

—*Have mercy upon us.*

That it may please Thee to convert and pardon all who disbelieve Thy threatenings of eternal woe, and consciously or unconsciously cause any to disregard them:

That it may please Thee to forgive us all that has been light, profane, or careless, in our thoughts, words, and ways, as concerning eternal things, and all that may have encouraged the same in others:

That it may please Thee to keep continually in our ears the sound of Thy Fatherly warnings, that we may be both ashamed and afraid to offend Thee; and do Thou often recall to our minds the thought, "What if I should be lost, and lose my Saviour for ever?"

That it may please Thee to grant unto us a deep sense of Thy mysterious love, for the quieting of all scruples, doubts, or misgivings, which the craft of the devil or man, or the infirmity of our nature, may at any time work within us:

That it may please Thee now and always, in all our trials, and in the trials of our Church and country, to guide, chasten, and uphold us by Thy good Spirit, and cause Thy warnings of everlasting death to become unto us words of eternal life:

V.

O Lamb of God,
>   Have mercy, and spare us.
>   Have mercy, and hear us.
>   Have mercy, and save us.

Antiph. Yet a little while is the Light with you: walk while ye have the Light, lest darkness come upon you: for he that walketh in darkness knoweth not whither he goeth.

V. I remembered Thine everlasting judgments, O Lord;
R. And received comfort.

I am horribly afraid
>   *For the ungodly that forsake Thy law.*

While ye have the Light, believe in the Light;
>   *That ye may be the children of Light.*

Jesus said, Father, forgive them;
>   *For they know not what they do.*

Yet a little while.

Collect. O Jesus, Who hast made known to Thy servants another death besides that which separates the soul from the body; deliver us not, we beseech Thee, into the bitter pangs of eternal death. And that we, with all those for whom we are bound to pray, may escape the sad sentence of final separation from Thee; grant us, we beseech Thee, courageous and dutiful hearts, truly and lovingly to accept Thy most true and merciful warnings: keep this Church and nation from believing a lie, and from denying or doubting any part of Thy Gospel; and perfect in us the love of the truth, that we may be saved through Thy merits and mediation, Who livest with the Father and the Holy Ghost, one God, world without end. *Amen.*

The Lord bless us, and keep us. The Lord make His face to shine upon us, and be gracious unto us. The Lord lift up His countenance upon us, and give us peace, both now and evermore. *Amen.*

www.ingramcontent.com/pod-product-compliance
Lightning Source LLC
Chambersburg PA
CBHW030709110426
42739CB00031B/1518